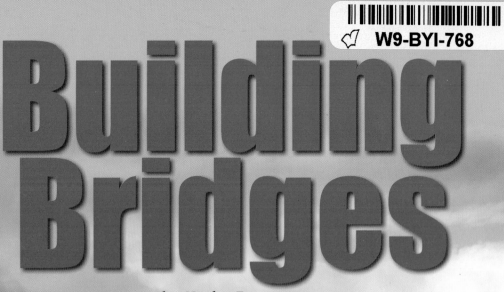

Building Bridges

by Kathy Furgang

TABLE OF CONTENTS

Introduction

On a hike through the woods, you come across a small stream. How can you cross it without getting wet? Build a **bridge**! The first bridges in th world were probably logs placed across streams.

A bridge **engineer** would call the top of the log the roadway of the bridge. It is the part of the bridge on which traffic travels. Every bridge, no matter how small or large, no matter how simple or complex, has a roadway.

In this book you will learn about five types of bridges. You will find out how they are built, how they work, and how people designed them.

beam bridge

arch bridge

movable
bridge

cable-stayed
bridge

suspension bridge

The strength needed for a bridge depends on the type of traffic that will cross it.

Beam Bridges

Beam bridges are the simplest bridges, the ones most like a log across a stream. The bridge in the photograph is a beam bridge. Builders sank two wooden **piers** (PEERZ) in the river to support the bridge. Then they set the beam in place from one bank to the other between the piers. Finally, they laid the roadway on top of the beam. This is the basic design of all beam bridges. The piers support the bridge and everything on it.

Piers support a roadway on a beam bridge by resisting the downward force of gravity.

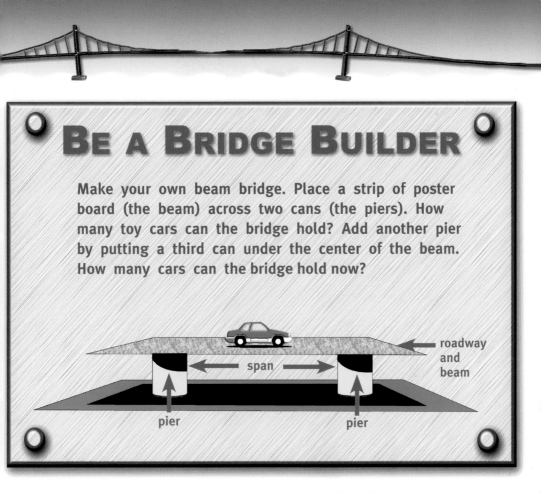

BE A BRIDGE BUILDER

Make your own beam bridge. Place a strip of poster board (the beam) across two cans (the piers). How many toy cars can the bridge hold? Add another pier by putting a third can under the center of the beam. How many cars can the bridge hold now?

roadway and beam

span

pier   pier

Bridge builders must know exactly how much weight a bridge can hold. Weight is a measure of the **force** of gravity. This force pulls downward on a bridge. The beam bridge's piers resist the force of gravity.

Weight makes the beam bend. If the distance between piers is too great, the beam may bend so much that it breaks. This distance is called the **span**. Most other types of bridges are designed to make the span longer and keep the beam from bending.

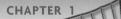

CHAPTER 1

The Lake Pontchartrain Causeway Bridge in New Orleans, Louisiana, is a beam bridge. The span of a beam bridge must be kept short, so engineers joined many short spans to make the longest over-water bridge in the world!

The Lake Pontchartrain Causeway Bridge is 24 miles (38.6 kilometers) long. The bridge has 2,243 spans!

In the late 1960s, engineers built a second bridge alongside the first bridge. Now each direction of traffic travels on a separate roadway. The two bridges connect in seven places. The connections allow vehicles to switch between the roadways when traffic is heavy in one direction.

IT'S A FACT!

Engineers strengthen beam bridges by adding to the basic design. They can add sections of steel in a pattern of triangles to stiffen the beam. This added part is called a truss. They can also add arms reaching out from the piers to help support the beam. These arms are called cantilevers (KANT-uh-LEE-verz).

This railroad bridge in Russia is a truss bridge.

The Forth Bridge in Scotland is a cantilever bridge.

Arch Bridges

Arch bridges are strong and solid. An arch is a curved shape that is naturally strong. It allows a longer span than a simple beam bridge. The downward force on the roadway follows along the arch. When the force reaches the end supports, or **abutments** (uh-BUT-ments), they resist it. The arch shape is especially good for crossing rivers because it leaves room for boats to go under the bridge.

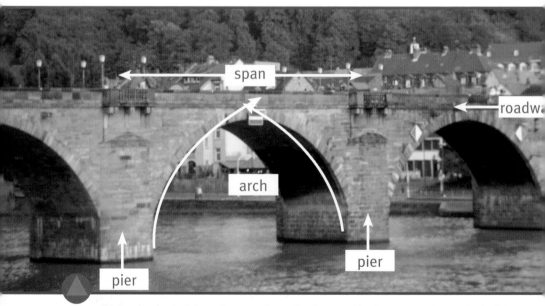

This arch bridge is made of stone. Today, most arch bridges are made of steel or concrete.

abutment

Iron Bridge once carried coal, iron, and limestone across the Severn River. Today, it is used only as a walkway.

People have been building arch bridges for more than 5,200 years. In ancient China, an arch bridge was built out of wood and rope woven from strips of bamboo. Today's engineers still study its design although the bridge is no longer standing.

The first arch bridge made of metal was built in Shropshire, England, in 1779. The 100-foot (30-meter) bridge became so famous that it was known around the world simply as Iron Bridge. It still stands today.

IT'S A FACT!

If steel had not been invented in the late 1800s, some of today's strongest, longest, and tallest bridges would never have been built. Steel is made by adding carbon to melted iron. Steel is stronger, lighter, and longer lasting than iron.

The New River, located in Fayetteville, West Virginia, has a steep gorge, or canyon. The gorge made travel very difficult until the New River Gorge Bridge was built. The bridge made it possible to cross the gorge in about a minute.

At 3,030 feet (909 meters), the bridge is the second-longest steel single-arch bridge in the world. The solid mountains on each side of the gorge are abutments for the arch. They provide the strength that allows the arch to be so long.

The New River Gorge Bridge rises 876 feet (265 meters) over the New River.

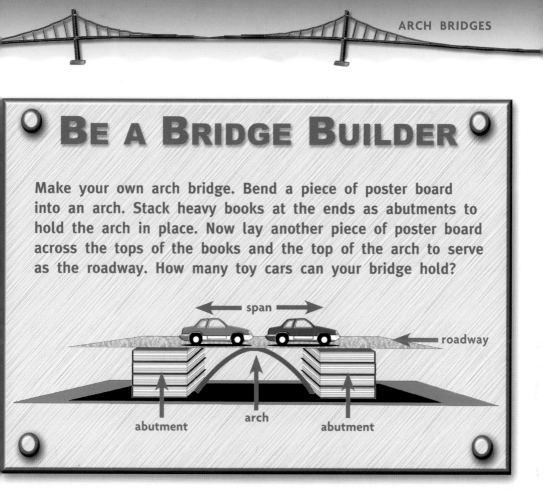

BE A BRIDGE BUILDER

Make your own arch bridge. Bend a piece of poster board into an arch. Stack heavy books at the ends as abutments to hold the arch in place. Now lay another piece of poster board across the tops of the books and the top of the arch to serve as the roadway. How many toy cars can your bridge hold?

span

roadway

abutment   arch   abutment

Although the solid mountains on each side of the gorge would become the abutments, temporary towers were put up to help with the bridge construction. Builders used the towers to run cables across the gorge. Then they brought sections of the bridge over the gorge on trolleys that ran along the cables.

Building the bridge took three years. The weight of all the steel used for the bridge was about 88 million pounds. That's heavier than 29,000 mid-size cars!

Movable Bridges

Castle drawbridges were the first movable bridges. The bridge was raised to keep people out of the castle or lowered to let them in.

Today's movable bridges allow tall ships to pass beyond the bridge. Movable bridges move up and down, swing from side to side, or split in the middle and lift. Some float on water. Traffic on a movable bridge must stop while the bridge moves.

In this vertical lift bridge, the center span moves up and down, much as an elevator does.

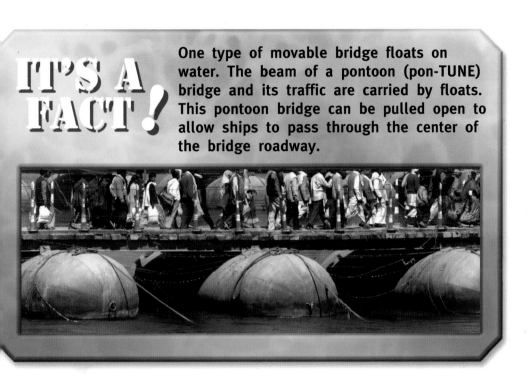

IT'S A FACT!

One type of movable bridge floats on water. The beam of a pontoon (pon-TUNE) bridge and its traffic are carried by floats. This pontoon bridge can be pulled open to allow ships to pass through the center of the bridge roadway.

A swing bridge moves to allow a ship to pass on a river. It rotates around a point in the center of the bridge. Swing bridges take up a lot of room and can take a long time to finish changing positions.

The vertical lift bridge has become more popular than the swing bridge. It works like an elevator. Part of the bridge roadway moves up and out of the way. A vertical lift bridge takes up less space than a swing bridge. And it can rise to different heights, depending on the height of the ship passing under it.

In the late 1800s, London, England, was a growing city on the Thames (TEMZ) River. Its streets and shipping ports were busy, yet the city had only one bridge. Pedestrians and vehicles had to travel hours out of their way to get to the bridge in order to cross the river. So work began on the design of Tower Bridge. More than 50 designs were considered before one was chosen. It had high overhead walkways for pedestrians and a roadway for vehicles. The roadway could be raised to allow ships to pass. More than 400 workers took eight years to build the bridge.

The 800-foot Tower Bridge was completed in 189

span

walkway

roadway

pier

pier

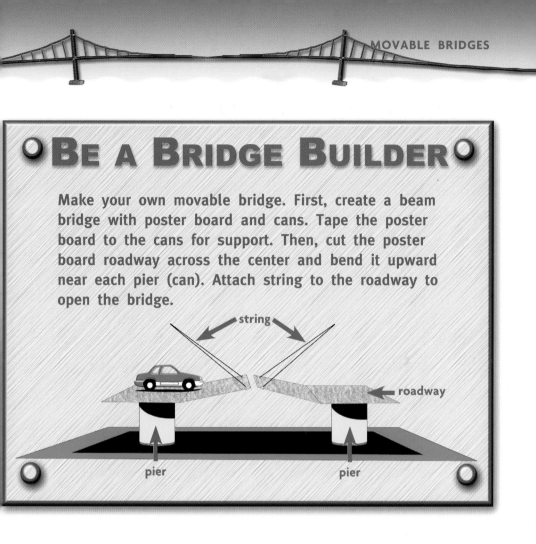

BE A BRIDGE BUILDER

Make your own movable bridge. First, create a beam bridge with poster board and cans. Tape the poster board to the cans for support. Then, cut the poster board roadway across the center and bend it upward near each pier (can). Attach string to the roadway to open the bridge.

string

roadway

pier   pier

Two piers were sunk into the bottom of the river to provide support. Steel was used for the framework of the walkway and piers.

The roadway of Tower Bridge splits in the middle. Each side lifts up so that ships can pass through. Bridges that open this way are called bascule (BASS-kyool) bridges. The word *bascule* comes from the French word for seesaw.

Suspension Bridges

In a suspension bridge, the roadway is attached to cables that hang from above. These cables run upward to larger cables that are attached to massive towers. The towers support the bridge.

The suspension design is especially good for an area where earthquakes occur. Because the bridge can sway and move, it's less likely to be damaged by the shock of an earthquake.

The Akashi Kaikyo (uh-KAH-shee KAY-kee-yoh) Bridge in Kobe, Japan, is a long and beautiful suspension bridge. Earthquakes often strike Kobe and the surrounding area.

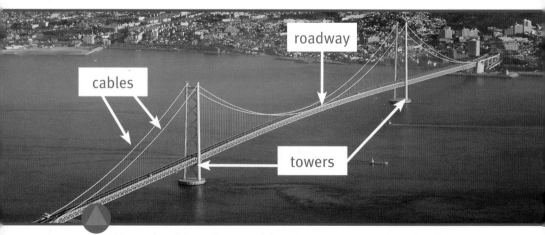

cables

roadway

towers

The Akashi Kaikyo Bridge is a suspension bridge.

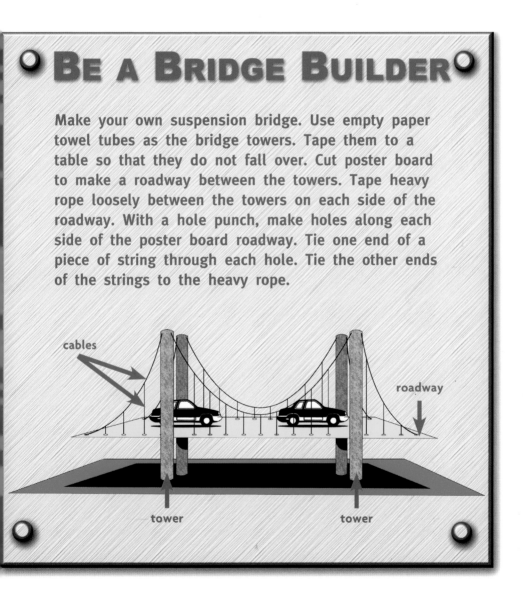

The bridge was completed in 1998. The Akashi Kaikyo Bridge is now the longest and tallest suspension bridge in the world. The longest single span is 6,527 feet (1,958 meters).

BE A BRIDGE BUILDER

Make your own suspension bridge. Use empty paper towel tubes as the bridge towers. Tape them to a table so that they do not fall over. Cut poster board to make a roadway between the towers. Tape heavy rope loosely between the towers on each side of the roadway. With a hole punch, make holes along each side of the poster board roadway. Tie one end of a piece of string through each hole. Tie the other ends of the strings to the heavy rope.

cables

roadway

tower

tower

The Tacoma Narrows Bridge across Puget Sound in Washington was designed to be very flexible. It turned out to be too flexible.

On November 7, 1940, a storm with strong winds struck the bridge. The bridge twisted in the wind for hours. The violent twisting strained the bridge enough to make it collapse. Fortunately, no lives were lost in the collapse.

These pictures show the violent twisting that eventually made the roadway of the Tacoma Narrows Bridge break apart and collapse

IT'S A FACT!

Building the Brooklyn Bridge

New York City's Brooklyn Bridge is one of the world's most famous bridges. Designed in 1869 by John A. Roebling, the bridge was not completed until 1883. Building it was dangerous work. It cost the lives of 27 workers. One of the first to die was designer Roebling. He was killed in an accident during the final planning stages. His son, Washington Roebling, took over.

Crews had to work underwater to build the foundations for the towers that supported the span. So the workers first sank watertight containers, called caissons (KAY-sahn), to the bottom of the river. These caissons provided a place for the crews to work underwater.

Bridge builders worked long hours in caissons deep beneath the East River. Many suffered because the pressure around their bodies changed too quickly when they went in and out of the caissons. Some workers died.

Caisson disease left Washington Roebling deaf and unable to walk. But he wouldn't give up work on the project! He supervised from his bedroom window in Brooklyn, where he could watch the bridge construction. His wife, Emily, gave orders to the workers for him.

Cable-Stayed Bridges

A cable-stayed bridge is quite similar to a suspension bridge. But the cables attach the roadway directly to the towers. This is the newest type of bridge design. One of the most spectacular cable-stayed bridges is the Sunshine Skyway Bridge in Tampa Bay, Florida.

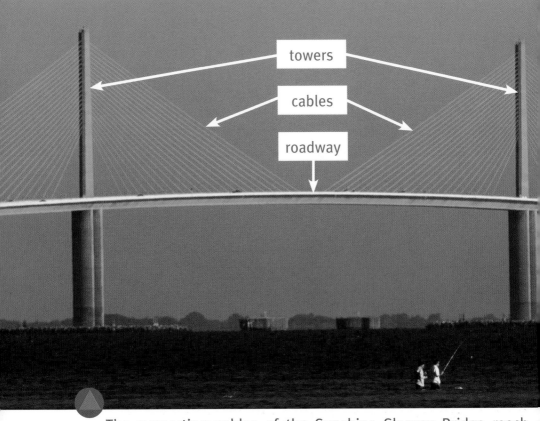

towers

cables

roadway

The supporting cables of the Sunshine Skyway Bridge reach directly down to the roadway from two tall piers.

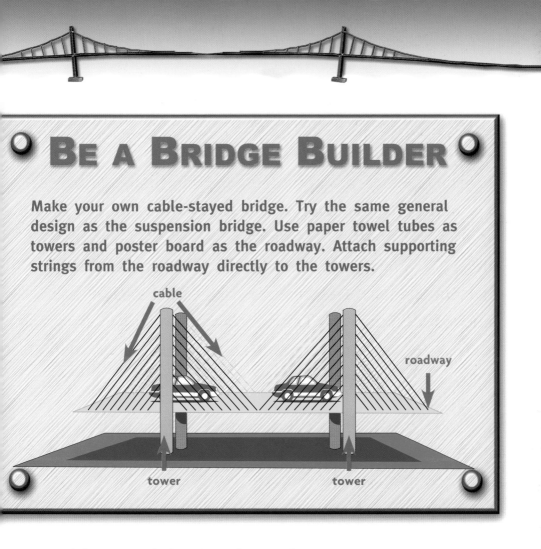

BE A BRIDGE BUILDER

Make your own cable-stayed bridge. Try the same general design as the suspension bridge. Use paper towel tubes as towers and poster board as the roadway. Attach supporting strings from the roadway directly to the towers.

cable

roadway

tower

tower

A cable-stayed bridge has advantages over a suspension bridge built to cover the same distance. The cable-stayed bridge will need less cable and it can be built quicker. Those advantages make a cable-stayed bridge less expensive than a suspension bridge in most cases. Many people find that cable-stayed bridges have a very striking modern look that makes them beautiful.

Conclusion

The Akashi Kaikyo Bridge may seem quite unlike a log across a stream. Yet both have the same essential features that make a bridge. Every bridge you have read about in this book has a roadway that carries traffic, a span, and a means of support. In the years since the first log across a stream was built, engineers have worked to make the span longer and longer.

What will the future bring? It's a good guess that a bridge longer and taller than any we've seen so far will be constructed!

✓ POINT

Picture It

What do you think a bridge of the future will look like? Using the descriptions of the bridges you have read about, design a futuristic bridge. Share your design with the group.

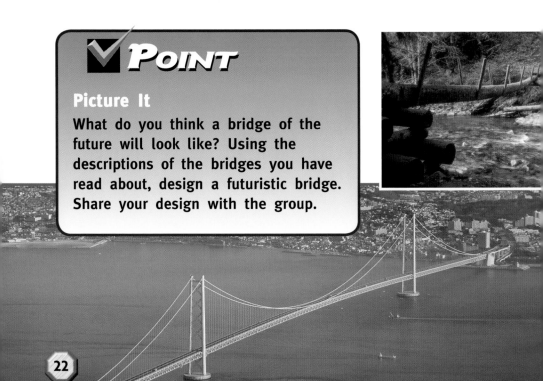

Glossary

abutment   (uh-BUT-ment) a massive structure supporting and resisting the downward force exerted on an arch (page 8)

bridge   (BRIJ) a structure that connects two locations above ground (page 2)

caisson   (KAY-sahn) a dry, watertight compartment that allows people to work underwater (page 19)

engineer   (en-jih-NEER) a person who designs machines or buildings (page 2)

force   (FORS) a push or a pull (page 5)

pier   (PEER) a vertical support, or post (page 4)

span   (SPAN) the distance between two supports on a bridge (page 5)

Index